# Let's Pop, Pop, POPCORN!

Written by Cynthia Schumerth

Illustrated by Mary Reaves Uhles

PUBLISHED BY SLEEPING BEAR PRESS

Dig the ground up with a hoe.

Plant the seeds and hope they grow.

Sunshine warms them in the earth.

Raindrops fall to quench their thirst.

# SURPRISE!

Like magic,
sprouts appear!

Green and tender,
finally here.

Every day we pull the weeds.

Protecting plants
we've grown from seeds.

waist high,

Knee high,

past our heads.

Ears sprout hair that's fuzzy red.

Pick before
the frost arrives.

Shuck them clean so each one dries.

Plink, plunk, plink,                    then find a pot.

Heat those kernels
good and hot.

Steam builds around each kernel's germ,
puffs the starch called endosperm.

The shells (called pericarps) explode!

First one POP!

POP POP POP! POP!

Then pops galore!

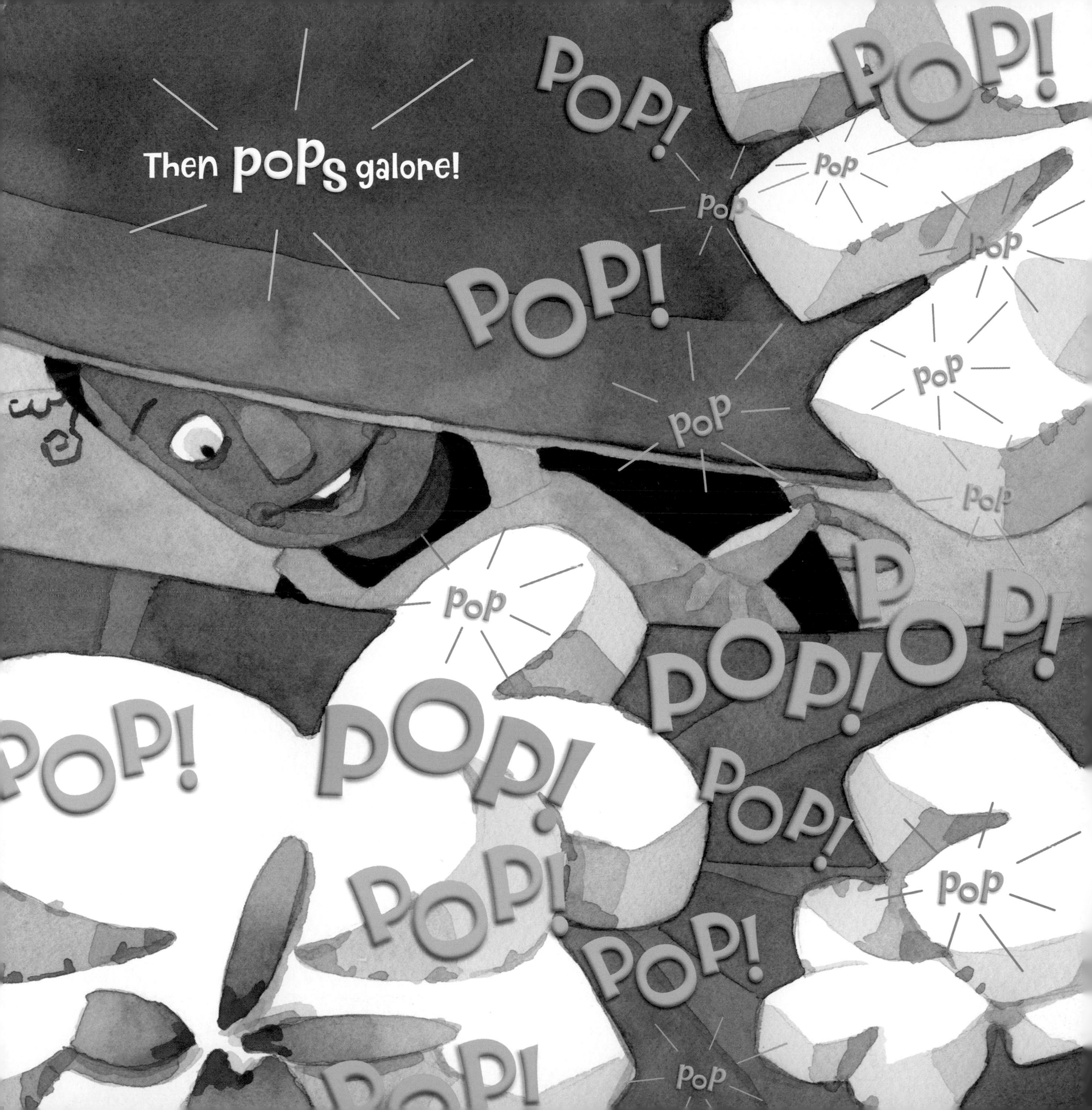

The popping stops—the work is done.

Now it's time for popcorn fun!

Lick our fingers—

**Mmm!
Delish!**

# Let's Get Popping!

Popcorn might just be America's favorite snack. It's fun, affordable, and tastes great. So let's make some!

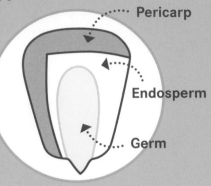

But first, let's learn about corn. There are four basic types of corn: dent corn, for feeding livestock; flint corn, also called Indian corn, and used mostly for decoration; sweet corn, also known as corn on the cob; and popcorn. The makeup of popcorn is what makes it special. Each kernel has three parts. The **pericarp**, or hull, protects the endosperm and germ inside the kernel. The **endosperm** is made up of starch and a small amount of water. The water in the endosperm is essential for the kernel to pop. The starch in the endosperm is the food for the germ. The **germ** is the living part of the kernel. If the seed is planted, it's the germ that will grow into a popcorn plant.

# Why Popcorn Pops!

When the popcorn kernel is heated, the moisture in the endosperm turns into steam. This steam softens the starch of the endosperm, making it expand. As the starch expands, it pushes against the inside of the kernel until the hull explodes with a POP. All this pressure causes the kernel to turn itself inside out. The hull ends up on the inside of the puffy white starch, which is what we see and call *popcorn*. A popped kernel will end up 40 to 50 times larger than it started. If the outer hull of the kernel is cracked before popping, the moisture inside can escape and the kernel will dry out. These kernels won't pop. The un-popped kernels that are left after popping are called *old maids*.

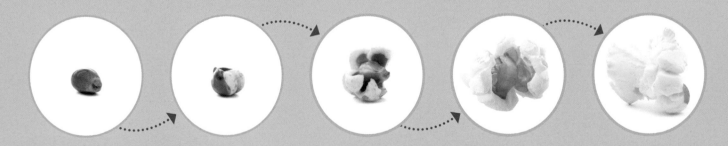

Popcorn comes in two shapes: snowflake and mushroom. Snowflake is the shape you'll see if you get popcorn at a ball game or at a movie theater. Mushroom-shaped popcorn is used for confectionary (*sweet*) treats like caramel corn, or for making popcorn balls.

**Snowflake**  **Mushroom**

# From Seed To Sprout
## SCIENCE ACTIVITY

**You'll need:** 10–12 popcorn kernels, 1 quart-size plastic ziplock bag, 1 paper towel, water

**Directions:**

1. Fold the paper towel to make several layers so it fits in the bag.
2. Wet the paper towel with water (it should be damp but not dripping).
3. Lay the kernels on the paper towel; don't overcrowd them.
4. Slide the wet paper towel with seeds facing up in the bag and seal the bag.
5. Place the bag in a warm spot but out of direct sunlight.
6. Check your seeds daily and look for (*observe*) any changes.
7. Make sure that the paper towel stays moist but is not dripping wet.
8. Seeds should begin to grow (*germinate*) in 3–12 days.

**Here's the science:** Every seed of popcorn contains everything it needs to grow into a plant. There is the germ, which is the baby plant; the endosperm, which is the food for the baby plant; and the pericarp, or hull, which protects them. All they need to start growing is water and a warm place to rest. The water softens the hull, allowing moisture inside the seed, which turns the starch in the endosperm into sugar. This sends a message to the baby plant that it's time to start growing. The baby plant uses the endosperm's sugar for food, giving it the energy it needs to grow. When it's strong enough, the baby plant pushes through the softened hull. This process is called *germination*.

You can plant your germinated seeds in your garden or in a pot with dirt and start growing your own popcorn plant. Make sure the pot has sunlight and water . . . but not too much; you don't want to drown your plant.

# Just For Fun!
## POPCORN SHEEP ART PROJECT

**You'll need:** 1 paper plate (any size), 1 sheet of black construction paper, glue, popped popcorn

1. From the construction paper, cut out the shape of a sheep's head (including its neck) and then cut out two sheep legs.
2. Glue the head to the side edge of the paper plate and then glue the legs to the bottom of the paper plate. This is your sheep.
3. Apply glue to one side of the paper plate, and then sprinkle it with the popcorn, covering the paper plate to make the sheep's wool.

*For John, Danielle, and David, you are my sunshine.*
*And for Mom and Dad, because you taught me to believe I could.*

Love, CS

✳

*For Jackson (Team Popcorn) and Grace (Team Chex Mix)*

—Mary

## SLEEPING BEAR PRESS™

2395 South Huron Parkway, Suite 200
Ann Arbor, MI 48104
www.sleepingbearpress.com

Printed and bound in the United States.

10 9 8 7 6 5 4 3 2 1

Library of Congress Cataloging-in-Publication Data

Names: Schumerth, Cynthia, author. | Uhles, Mary, 1972- illustrator.
Title: Let's pop, pop, popcorn! / written by Cynthia Schumerth ;
illustrated by Mary Reaves Uhles.
Description: Ann Arbor : Sleeping Bear Press, 2021. | Audience: Ages 4-8 |
Summary: "Told through rhyme, the step-by-step process of how America's
favorite snack is grown, harvested, and popped is explained. Back matter
includes scientific facts and activities"—Provided by publisher.
Identifiers: LCCN 2020031542 | ISBN 9781534110427 (hardcover)
Subjects: LCSH: Popcorn—Juvenile literature. | Cooking (Popcorn)—Juvenile literature.
Classification: LCC SB191.P64 S38 2021 | DDC 635/.677—dc23
LC record available at https://lccn.loc.gov/2020031542

Page 30 Credits: © Tribalium/Shutterstock.com; © Valentina Razumova/Shutterstock.com;
© George3973/Shutterstock.com; © Hortimages/Shutterstock.com